The **Ippolito** Legacy
Myth, Nobility, and New Worlds

L'eredità degli Ippolito:
mito, nobiltà e nuovi mondi

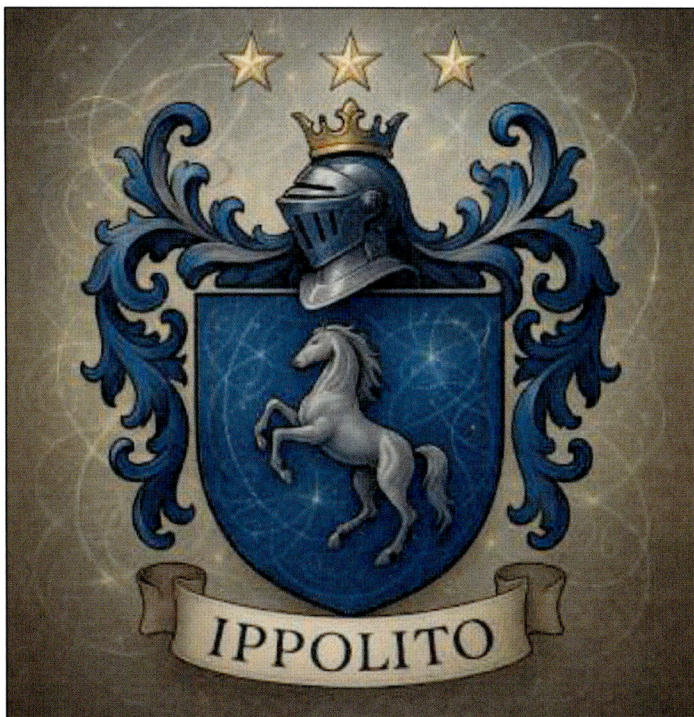

Heraldic Coat of Arms from its origins / Stemma Araldico dalle origini

A Comprehensive History and Celebration
of the Ippolito Family Surname

Una storia completa e celebrativa del cognome Ippolito

Di: Giuseppe Antonio Ippolito

📑 Una Nota al Lettore *Italiano*

(English follows)

È con profondo rispetto e un senso radicato di appartenenza al nostro retaggio che vi presento quest'opera. Essendo un orgoglioso discendente del cognome Ippolito, e di fatto, parte io stesso della vibrante diaspora Ippolito, sono nato e cresciuto negli Stati Uniti. Questo personale viaggio attraverso continenti e culture ha instillato in me un duplice apprezzamento sia per le mie radici italo-americane che per il ricco arazzo della nostra ascendenza italiana.

Questo libro, pertanto, trova la sua voce nella lingua inglese, non come un allontanamento dalle nostre origini, ma come un ponte attraverso gli oceani. La mia intenzione primaria nell'intraprendere quest'impresa è stata quella di intessere insieme i fili di questi due amati retaggi. Scrivendo in inglese, la mia sincera speranza è che questa narrazione possa raggiungere uno spettro più ampio della nostra famiglia Ippolito dispersa, consentendo a un maggior numero di individui all'interno della nostra diaspora globale di connettersi con la storia condivisa, lo spirito duraturo e il notevole viaggio di un nome che ha viaggiato dalle colline assolate d'Italia a innumerevoli nuovi orizzonti. Possa servire da testamento al nostro passato collettivo e da faro per il nostro futuro intrecciato.

📃 Nota para el Lector *Español*
(English follows)

Con profundo respeto y un profundo sentido de pertenencia a nuestra herencia, les presento esta obra. Como orgulloso descendiente del apellido Ippolito, y de hecho, parte de la vibrante diáspora Ippolito, nací y crecí en Estados Unidos. Este viaje personal a través de continentes y culturas me ha inculcado una doble apreciación por mis raíces italoamericanas y la rica herencia de nuestra ascendencia italiana.

Por lo tanto, este libro encuentra su voz en el idioma inglés, no como una desviación de nuestros orígenes, sino como un puente a través de océanos. Mi principal intención al emprender esta labor ha sido entrelazar los hilos de estos dos preciados legados. Escribiendo en inglés, mi sincera esperanza es que esta narrativa llegue a un espectro más amplio de nuestra dispersa familia Ippolito, permitiendo que más personas de nuestra diáspora global conecten con la historia compartida, el espíritu perdurable y la extraordinaria trayectoria de un nombre que ha viajado desde las soleadas colinas de Italia hacia innumerables nuevos horizontes. Que sirva como testimonio de nuestro pasado colectivo y un faro para nuestro futuro entrelazado.

Table of Contents

Poetic Invocation

Invocazione Poetica / Invocación Poética

"Behold, the Ippolito name, a beacon through time's swirling currents, bearing souls whose virtuous paths illuminate the shadows, each life a verse in a celestial song of enduring spirit and noble deed."

"Ecco, il nome Ippolito, faro tra i turbini del tempo, recante anime i cui sentieri virtuosi rischiarano le ombre, ogni vita un verso in un canto celeste di spirito duraturo e nobile azione."

"He aquí, el nombre Ippolito, un faro entre las corrientes arremolinadas del tiempo, portador de almas cuyos senderos virtuosos iluminan las sombras, cada vida un verso en un canto celestial de espíritu perdurable y obra noble."

Dedication

To Vincent and Helen Ippolito— My beloved
parents and guardians of our family's legacy,
To the grandparents who came before.
To Judith Ippolito, my late wife, and to all
Ippolitos—past, present, and future— Whose
stories weave together our shared history.

In loving memory of:

- ❖ Vincenzo Ippolito
  -Great grandfather

- ❖ Dominica Ippolito
  -Great grandmother

- ❖ (Giuseppe Antonio) Joseph Anthony
  Ippolito
  -Grandfather

- ❖ Elvira Pasqualina (Pisano) – Ippolito
  -Grandmother

- ❖ (Domenico Giuseppe) Michael Joseph
  Maccalous (Macaluso) *-Grandfather*

- ❖ Rosaria (Rose) Isabel Di Martino
  Maccalous *-Grandmother*

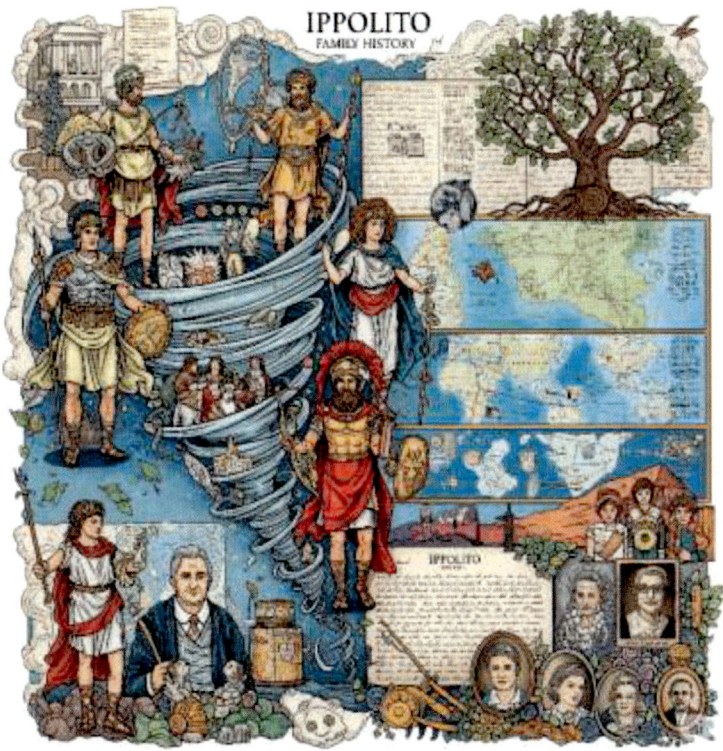

IPPOLITO
FAMILY HISTORY

Preface

This book is a heartfelt tribute to all who carry the Ippolito name, and to the countless ancestors whose courage, faith, and resilience echo through our family's story. May this narrative serve as both a window into the past and a bridge to future generations, preserving our shared heritage for years to come. It explores the ancient origins, the noble lines, the daily lives, and the migratory journeys that have shaped the Ippolito family across centuries and continents. Through historical accounts, cultural insights, and personal narratives, we aim to uncover the rich mosaic of experiences that define this enduring surname, celebrating its past while inspiring its future.

A Name Born of *Myth and Martyrdom*

Long before it graced church records and noble scrolls in Italy, the name Ippolito was born amidst the myths and marble temples of ancient Greece. There, the story of **Hippolytos** unfolded—a tale woven with threads of purity, unwavering devotion, cruel betrayal, and ultimate divine vindication. Hippolytos, the noble son of Theseus, the legendary king of Athens, was known for his exceptional beauty and his profound, almost ascetic devotion to Artemis, the goddess of the hunt, wilderness, and childbirth. He swore to live a life untouched by romantic entanglements, dedicating himself entirely to the wild freedom of the hunt and the sacred groves that were the domain of his chosen deity. His days were spent in forests, pursuing game with unmatched skill, shunning the trappings of courtly life and the company of women.

Statue of Hippolytus

Yet even the most virtuous are not shielded from tragedy, especially when entangled in the affairs of mortals and gods. His stepmother, Phaedra, consumed by an illicit passion for Hippolytos, found her advances rejected. In her despair and shame, she falsely accused him of an unspeakable sin, condemning him in the eyes of his father, Theseus. Believing his wife's lie, Theseus invoked a curse from Poseidon, his divine father, against his innocent son. Hippolytos met a brutal and agonizing death when, during a chariot ride along the coast, a monstrous sea-beast rose from the waves, startling his horses and dragging his chariot to ruin. Despite the horrific manner of his passing, in the end, the truth prevailed. Artemis herself intervened, revealing Phaedra's deception and clearing Hippolytos's name. His story became a poignant symbol of unwavering honor, the fragile nature of innocence amidst envy and desire, and the ultimate triumph of truth. For the ancient Greeks, Hippolytos embodied steadfastness and virtue, and his name resonated with a profound sense of integrity.

As centuries turned and the Roman Empire embraced a new faith, this mythic name found new life in the earliest days of Christianity. **Saint Hippolytus** of Rome, a learned theologian, prolific writer, and steadfast martyr of the early third century, carried forward the spirit of righteous endurance.

Born in the late 2nd century, possibly in Rome or the Near East, he became one of the most important Christian scholars of his time. He served as a presbyter in the Roman church and was a fierce defender of orthodox Christian doctrine against various heresies.

His extensive writings, including the *Apostolic Tradition*, provide invaluable insights into the liturgy, sacraments, and structure of the early Christian community. He was a contemporary of Pope Callixtus I, and a schism arose due to differing views on penance and church discipline, leading to Hippolytus being elected as an anti-pope by a dissenting faction.

Saint Ippolito

Despite this complex period, his unwavering faith during persecution led to his exile to the mines of Sardinia alongside Pope Pontian. There, they reconciled, and both died as martyrs, cementing Saint Hippolytus's legacy as a true hero of the faith. His faithfulness unto death inspired devotion throughout the Roman Empire and beyond, solidifying the name's association with strength, wisdom, and martyrdom. Thus, Hippolytos gracefully transformed into Ippolito—spoken in the warm, melodic dialects of Italy, carried proudly as both a cherished *given name* and a distinctive family *surname*, a living testament to a heritage spanning millennia from the philosophical purity of ancient Greece to the spiritual fortitude of early Christianity.

"Chi ha patria, ha tutto."

— Italian proverb

(He who has a homeland has everything.)

Roots in the *Heart of Italy*

As the ancient echoes of Hippolytos settled into legend, finding new resonance in the burgeoning Christian world, the name Ippolito found fertile soil and took deep root in the vibrant cities and rolling hills of Italy. By the Middle Ages, families proudly carrying this distinguished name had become integral to the living fabric of two distinct regions: Mantua in the northern Lombardy plain and Pistoia in the heart of Tuscany. These were not merely geographical locations but dynamic centers known for their profound cultural brilliance, strategic political intrigue, and burgeoning commerce.

Mantua, cradled by its encircling lakes and protected by formidable walls, was a veritable jewel of the Lombardy plain, a city-state renowned for its art and power. Here, Ippolito ancestors walked cobblestone streets alongside legendary poets, shrewd merchants, valiant soldiers, and influential noblemen.

Mantua & Pistoia

Historical records from the period, meticulously preserved in civic archives and ecclesiastical registers, speak of Ippolito family members serving as feudal counts, learned jurists, and trusted advisors who guided the city's affairs and pledged loyalty to the powerful Gonzaga family, who ruled Mantua for centuries and were great patrons of the arts. The Ippolitos contributed to Mantua's intellectual and administrative life, participating in the construction of its grand palaces and the shaping of its laws, their names appearing in various official decrees and land deeds. Their influence was particularly noted in civic administration and legal scholarship, contributing to the stability and prosperity of the region.

Simultaneously, in the picturesque landscapes of Tuscany, the ancient city of Pistoia, with its distinctive stone towers, venerable churches, and bustling markets, also bore witness to the rise of an early and prominent Ippolito lineage. This branch of the family thrived amidst the region's rich agricultural bounty. Families gathered beneath the dappled shade of ancient olive groves and sprawling vineyards that still grace the Tuscan hills today. Records from Pistoia often depict the Ippolitos as landowners, skilled artisans, and respected members of the local guilds, actively participating in the economic and social life of the community. They were known for their craftsmanship and their commitment to local traditions, their homes often becoming centers of community life.

Through strategic alliances, advantageous marriages, and periods of royal favor, the Ippolito branches proliferated and extended their influence across the peninsula. A pivotal moment in the family's geographical expansion occurred in the 13th century. When the formidable Holy Roman Emperor Frederick II, known as the *Stupor Mundi* (Wonder of the World), extended his vast influence into southern Italy, establishing his highly centralized kingdom in Sicily and Calabria, he entrusted loyal and capable families to settle and secure his kingdom's farthest reaches.

Holy Roman Emperor Frederick II

Among those who rode south with imperial backing, contributing to the establishment of new feudal territories and administrative structures, was Martino Ippolito. His family, already established in the north, would take root anew in the warm, fertile lands of Sicily and the rugged, sun-drenched region of Calabria. Here, grand castles overlooked sunlit valleys, their strategic positions speaking of power and defense, and the resonant peal of church bells called generations of Ippolitos to daily prayer, community gatherings, and joyous celebrations. Their names were not merely whispered but indelibly etched into stone lintels of ancestral homes, meticulously recorded in court registers, and lovingly inscribed in baptismal fonts, each record another vital thread in the intricate and enduring tapestry of our family's story, showcasing their enduring presence from the plains of Lombardy to the southern reaches of the Mediterranean.

Amidst this burgeoning milieu of family influence and migration across the Italian peninsula, another Ippolito, **Cardinal Ippolito de' Medici** (born on April 19, 1511, and died on August 10, 1535, at the age of 24), emerged as a figure of undeniable, albeit complex and at times controversial, stature. Yet, it was his magnificent legacy as a fervent patron of the arts that truly illuminated his path through history.

Cardinal Ippolito de' Medici

A man of profound aesthetic sensibility, he held an unyielding devotion to literature, music, and the visual arts, channeling his considerable wealth and formidable influence to champion a constellation of extraordinary talents. Among those who flourished under his generous wing were the masterful sculptor and goldsmith Benvenuto Cellini, the evocative painters Jacopo Pontormo and Agnolo Bronzino, the gifted composer Luca Marenzio, and the celebrated poet Torquato Tasso. Beyond individual patronage, Cardinal Ippolito's commitment to cultural flourishing culminated in the establishment of the illustrious *Accademia degli Infiammati* in Florence. This literary academy, dedicated to the rigorous study and eloquent promotion of the arts, became a pivotal crucible in the vibrant development of Renaissance humanism, its ideals radiating outward to inspire the burgeoning intellectual and creative spirit across Italy.

From the ancient whispers of a name that found its rebirth in the fertile soil of Italy, the Ippolito family, through centuries of dedication and daring, etched its indelible mark across the peninsula. From the hallowed streets of Mantua and the sun-drenched hills of Pistoia to the rugged beauty of Sicily and Calabria, our ancestors wove a rich and enduring narrative of resilience, influence, and profound cultural contribution. This legacy, rooted deep in the heart of Italy, continues to resonate through generations, a testament to the enduring spirit of the Ippolito name and the vibrant story that binds us all.

"Dio benedica questa casa e tutti quelli che vi entrano."

— Italian blessing
(May God bless this house and all who enter it.)

Ties of Nobility — *Heraldry and Noble Lines*

As the Ippolito family
established itself
firmly across Italy,
from the strategic
northern strongholds
of Mantua and Pistoia
to the sun-washed
southern territories of
Sicily and Calabria, the symbols they carried
came to reflect not only their growing noble
standing but also the profound values they held
dear. In an age when a coat of arms was far
more than mere decoration—it was a powerful
declaration of lineage, loyalty, and identity—the
Ippolito arms stood as a visual promise of
courage, virtue, and steadfast faith, a testament
to their earned prestige.

Among the most enduring and widely recognized
of these heraldic emblems is a majestic blue
shield, a color often associated with truth and

loyalty, graced by a magnificent golden lion. The lion, a venerable and ancient symbol across countless cultures, here represents bravery, fierce strength, and regal nobility. This silent, golden beast roars from centuries-old parchments, its image meticulously carved into the stone lintels of ancestral homes, and proudly displayed on marble plaques that have weathered the relentless passage of time. Above the lion, three six-pointed stars gleam,

IPPOLITO

often depicted in silver or gold, serving as celestial tokens of divine guidance, protection, and singular favor. They are constant, like the heavens above, symbolizing enduring hope and aspiration.

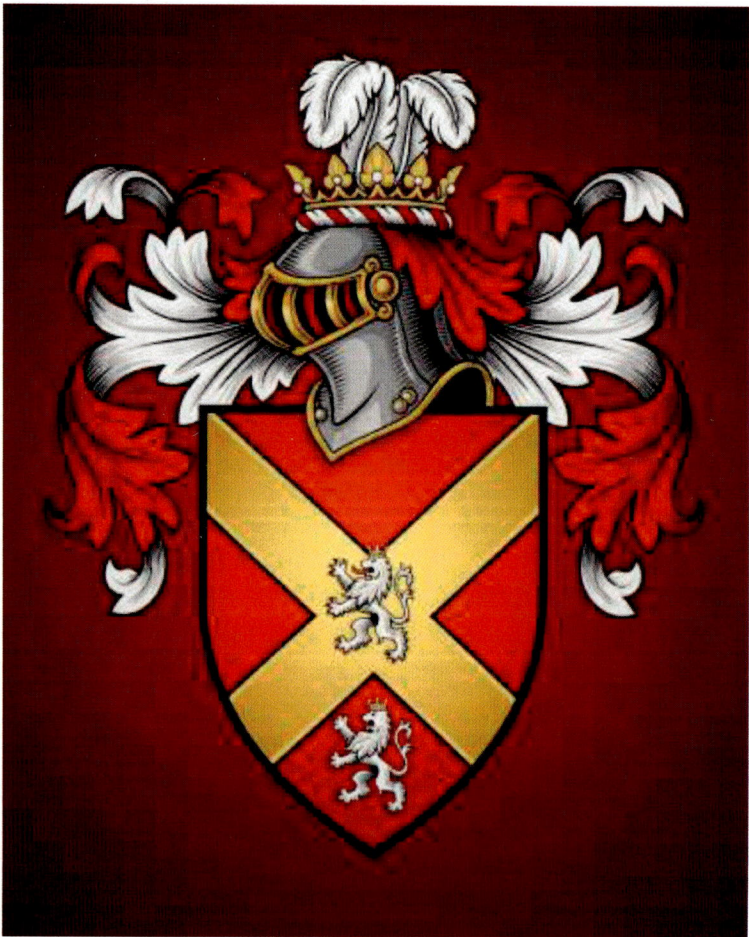

As various branches of the family spread and established themselves in different regions, interesting variants of the coat of arms began to appear, each reflecting unique regional affiliations or specific achievements. Some branches bore a striking red shield, a color often signifying magnanimity and valor, crossed with a bold golden band, perhaps indicative of a military achievement or a significant marriage. Other prestigious Ippolito lines proudly topped their arms with the powerful and majestic double-headed eagle, an undeniable imperial sign of unwavering fealty to the Holy Roman Emperor. This particular symbol not only denoted loyalty but also significant imperial recognition, suggesting land grants, titles, or high office bestowed by the Emperor himself.

Ippolito

In the quaint, sun-drenched villages of Calabria and on the expansive, ancient estates of Sicily, these carefully crafted symbols were far more than simple decoration—they were potent declarations of identity and legacy. They proclaimed that an Ippolito carried a heritage earned through valor on battlefields, wisdom in the hallowed courtrooms, and piety at sacred altars. The details within the arms often hinted at historical events: perhaps a particular lion indicated a brave ancestor's role in a siege, or a specific star arrangement commemorated a significant historical event that brought the family renown. These arms were displayed on banners during medieval tournaments, etched onto the family silver, and even woven into tapestries, serving as constant reminders of their esteemed position. To this very day, these ancient arms serve as powerful reminders that while a family name may pass effortlessly from father to son, or from mother to daughter, its profound honor and established prestige must be vigilantly safeguarded and continually reaffirmed in each new generation, ensuring that the legacy of courage and virtue continues to shine as brightly as the golden lion and the celestial stars.

While many families proudly display their coats of arms, it's important to understand that Italian heraldry, unlike some other traditions, often exhibits a remarkable fluidity. A single, definitive "family crest" rarely applies to all branches of a widespread Italian surname like Ippolito. Instead, variations emerged over centuries due to several factors:

Regional Differences: Heraldic traditions varied across Italy's numerous historical states and kingdoms. What was granted or adopted in Naples might differ from that in Mantua or Sicily.

Individual Grants and Achievements: Arms were frequently granted to individuals or specific branches for particular services, nobility, or achievements, rather than to an entire surname. These new grants often incorporated unique elements.

Marriage and Alliances: Through marriage, arms could be combined, quartered, or adapted, leading to new variations within family lines.

Adoption and Custom: Families might also adopt or subtly alter existing arms over time, reflecting their own history or simply through custom, especially in the absence of strict regulatory bodies that existed elsewhere.

This dynamic nature explains why you'll find "many variations of the Ippolito family crest." Each variant often tells a unique story about a specific branch, its geographical ties, or significant historical events in its lineage, providing a richer, more nuanced understanding of the family's diverse legacy.

"Fortis cadere, cedere non potest."
— Latin proverb
(The brave may fall, but cannot yield.)

Daily Life in the *Homeland*

While the grand narratives of history meticulously preserve noble titles, impressive heraldic scrolls, and significant military feats, it was truly in the bustling kitchens, the sun-drenched vineyards, and the lively village squares that the authentic, vibrant heartbeat of the Ippolito family pulsed rhythmically through the centuries. This was where the legacy was not just recorded but lived, breathed, and passed down.

In the rolling, verdant hills of Calabria, a region renowned for its rugged beauty and agricultural abundance, the Ippolito families cultivated the land with deep respect and tireless effort. Olive groves, centuries old, offered their liquid gold—a staple of the Mediterranean diet and a significant source of income. Citrus orchards, heavy with oranges, lemons, and bergamot, perfumed the air with their sweet, tangy scent,

contributing to both the family table and local markets. The rhythms of life were dictated by the seasons: the olive harvest, the grape stomp, the gathering of wild herbs from the hillsides. Family members worked together, from the youngest children helping to gather olives to the eldest women preparing the day's meals, fostering a profound sense of unity and shared purpose.

Let's take a moment to explore a lasting and fascinating chapter of the Ippolito family's enduring legacy, one that beautifully intertwines with the very soul of Calabria's winemaking heritage. It is here, in the sun-kissed embrace of *Cirò Marina*, that the **Ippolito** name takes on a vibrant, living form through the **oldest continuously operating winery in Calabria**, established with pride in **1845**. This remarkable estate, with its 250 acres of vineyards, is a testament to generations of Ippolito passion, cultivating almost exclusively the indigenous grape varieties that thrive from the dreamy hilly hinterland to the picturesque coastal plains.

Today, this proud branch of our family Ippolito family looks back with immense pride on this rich history, their accumulated wisdom ensuring that the profound relationship between history, vine, soil, and human touch continues to flourish.

Ippolito 1845, *the oldest still operating winery in Calabria, Italy*
Artist's rendition by: Giuseppe Ippolito 2025

Meanwhile, in Sicily's coastal towns and fertile interior, the daily life of the Ippolitos was equally vibrant, shaped by the island's unique blend of cultures and its bountiful sea. The scent of fresh-caught fish grilling over open flames mingled with the rich aroma of sun-dried tomatoes, robust garlic, and fragrant basil, creating an unforgettable culinary tapestry that defined the island's character. Here, fishing was a way of life for many, while others cultivated wheat, almonds, and pistachios. The Ippolitos of Sicily were often skilled farmers, fishermen, or artisans, contributing their talents to the island's economy and cultural richness.

Across both regions, a central ritual of Ippolito family life revolved around the table. Families gathered at long, sturdy wooden tables, often handmade and passed down through generations, to share simple yet exquisitely flavored meals. Bread, freshly baked and still warm, was dipped into golden olive oil produced from their own trees. Toasts were offered with glasses of homemade wine, pressed from grapes nurtured on ancestral lands, each sip a taste of their heritage. Children learned early the stories of saints and heroes, listened intently to family lore, and absorbed the proper words for blessings before a meal, embedding faith and respect into their earliest memories. Sunday Mass was not merely an obligation but a cornerstone of community life, a time for spiritual nourishment and social connection.

Speaking of spiritual nourishment, and adding another layer to the Ippolito legacy, we turn our gaze to the serene **Sant'Ippolito hill**, nestled gracefully near the historic town of Caltagirone, Sicily. This particular place holds a special resonance for those who cherish history, as it is renowned for its significant archaeological discoveries. Imagine, beneath the quiet earth of this hill, lie whispers of ancient civilizations and untold stories, waiting to be unearthed. It's a place where the past quite literally rises to meet the present, offering glimpses into lives lived long ago and enriching our understanding of the broader historical landscape surrounding the Ippolito name. This tranquil hill stands as a silent testament to the deep roots and widespread influence of the Ippolito family, reminding us that their heritage is not just about individuals, but also about the very ground upon which history unfolded.

Sant'Ippolito hill / Caltagirone, in Sicily

Village festivals, vibrant and joyous, transformed the squares into celebrations of harvest, saints' days, and family milestones, weaving faith and community into the very fabric of everyday existence. These gatherings were loud, passionate, and filled with the warmth of shared kinship.

For the Ippolitos, work and worship, celebration and sorrow, were not separate spheres but intimately interwoven threads of a single, vibrant tapestry. They sowed their fields with the hope of abundant harvests, weathered periods of war, famine, and hardship with quiet strength and an unyielding resilience, and marked baptisms and weddings with joyous laughter that echoed against the ancient church walls, standing firm for centuries. Even today, visitors to these charming, historic towns can walk the same ancient streets, feel the worn cobblestones beneath their feet, hear the familiar church bells tolling across tiled roofs, and taste the authentic recipes handed down through countless generations—a direct, delicious link to those first Ippolito kitchens, reminding us of the enduring legacy of daily life in the homeland.

"A tavola non si invecchia."
— Italian proverb
(At the table, one does not grow old.)

Winds of Change — *Migration to the New World*

No family name, however ancient or rooted, journeys through centuries without encountering the profound, often bittersweet tide of migration. For the Ippolito clan, this tide rose powerfully and irrevocably in the late 19th and early 20th centuries, a period of immense global demographic shifts. Driven by a complex interplay of overwhelming hunger, pervasive political turmoil, and the universal, alluring dream of prosperity and a better life, thousands upon thousands of Italians, including many Ippolitos, were compelled to push toward unknown horizons, leaving behind the familiar comforts of their ancestral lands for distant, often daunting, shores.

Imagine an Ippolito farmer, perhaps named Giuseppe, residing in a small, stone house nestled on the sunbaked outskirts of Palermo, Sicily. As escalating taxes levied by a newly unified, often indifferent, Italian government climbed, and as his small plot of farmland yielded increasingly meager harvests, barely enough to feed his growing family, the burden became unbearable. One evening, beneath the cooling shade of a gnarled fig tree, he gathered his wife, Maria, and their children, whispering the fateful plan: they would leave. They would sell what little they had, pool their meager savings, and embark on the perilous journey to America, a land promising opportunity. In Naples, a young, ambitious mason named Vincenzo Ippolito, whose family had faced generations of economic hardship, queued anxiously at the bustling port. Clutched tightly in his calloused hand was a precious, crumpled steamship ticket, and in his other, a small, intricately carved wooden rosary, a poignant farewell gift from his tearful mother. On that same crowded, chaotic dock, children named Rosa, Giuseppe, and Maria, too young to fully grasp the enormity of their departure, wept silently, holding tight to their father's strong, work-worn hand, their innocent eyes filled with a mixture of fear and wonder, unsure whether the vast, churning ocean ahead would deliver them to boundless promise or heartbreaking disillusionment. The emotional weight of these departures was immense, marked by tearful goodbyes and the silent promise to never forget their homeland.

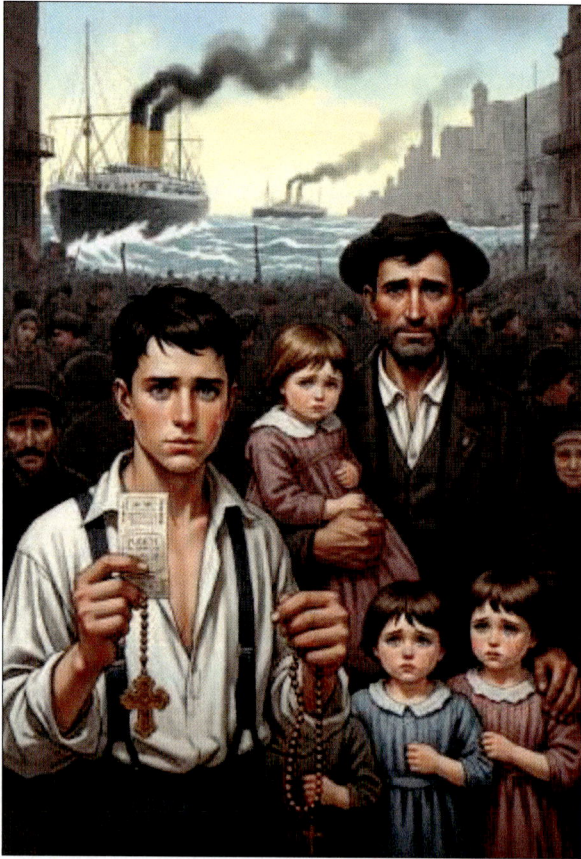

Leaving Italy for a new life.

Italian immigrants arriving to America

Their ships—initially tall-masted sailing schooners reliant on wind, later transitioning to the magnificent, smoke-belching steam-driven giants of the industrial age—churned relentlessly through furious storms and across vast expanses of salty, unforgiving ocean. For weeks, they endured cramped, unsanitary steerage conditions, battling seasickness, fear, and the gnawing uncertainty of their future. Finally, after an arduous journey, they sighted the iconic Statue of Liberty, a beacon of hope, before arriving at Ellis Island's imposing granite halls, the gateway to their new lives. There, under the echoing arches of the immense immigration depot, where countless languages blended into a discordance of dreams and anxieties, the name Ippolito was often meticulously written and sometimes, due to mispronunciation or clerical error, re-written by customs clerks. It might be unintentionally twisted into unfamiliar forms like Eppolito or Hipolito, or even anglicized entirely. Yet, despite these superficial changes, the essence of the name, its profound history, and the collective memory it embodied, remained unchanged and deeply cherished in the bearer's resilient heart.

In the bustling, burgeoning boroughs of New York City, the newly arrived Ippolitos joined the vibrant chorus of millions of other immigrants. They labored tirelessly, building the very railroads that would connect a burgeoning nation, raising the walls of the towering tenements that would house future generations, and opening small, tenacious neighborhood bakeries and groceries fragrant with the comforting aroma of fresh bread, aromatic garlic, and tomatoes simmered slowly with sweet basil.

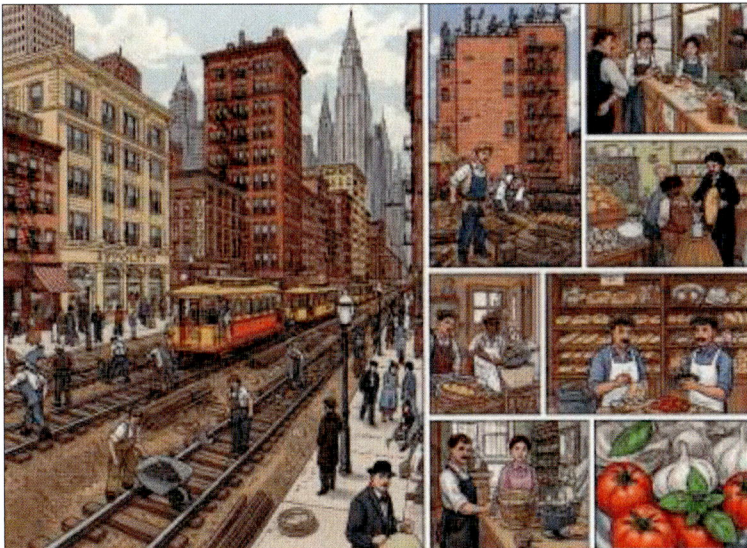

Italian immigrants building a new future.

These small businesses became vital community hubs, offering a taste of home. Some Ippolitos ventured even farther afield, chasing opportunities wherever they arose: to the dark, dangerous coal mines of Pennsylvania, providing the fuel for America's industrial might; to Chicago's sprawling, grimy stockyards, where new fortunes were made; to the sun-drenched vineyards of California, cultivating the land much as their ancestors had in Italy; or even across the equator to Argentina's incredibly fertile Pampas, a vast expanse of land that, like the name they bore, promised abundant new life and endless possibilities.

These brave pioneers endured immense hardship: cramped and often unsanitary lodgings, back-breaking labor for meager wages, and the stinging, isolating loneliness of navigating a new world with an unfamiliar tongue and different customs. They faced discrimination and hardship with remarkable fortitude. Yet, amidst these struggles, they clung fiercely to their cultural heritage. Every Sunday, the familiar, comforting peal of church bells reminded them of the piazzas they had left behind. Festivals, vibrant with music, dance, and traditional foods, bloomed on urban streets, transforming harsh realities into moments of joyous community. Music, often mournful yet resilient, drifted from open windows, and the melodious laughter of children learning two languages at once—Italian and English, or Italian and Spanish—filled the narrow alleys and bustling city squares. From one generation to the next, fueled by perseverance and an unwavering sense of family, the Ippolito name found firm and enduring roots in this new soil— an undeniable echo of the old world's enduring spirit, now singing its vibrant, new song in a new land, contributing to the rich multicultural fabric of their adopted homes.

"Chi va piano, va sano e va lontano."

— Italian proverb
(He who goes slowly, goes safely and goes far.)

The Ippolitos Today — *Notable Stories*

Time, vast oceans, and ever-changing frontiers have emphatically not dulled the intrinsic vitality of the Ippolito spirit. Instead, this resilient and adaptable essence has found myriad new expressions, vibrant new voices, and remarkable new triumphs across every continent, showcasing the enduring legacy of a name rooted in ancient myth and medieval nobility. The diverse achievements of contemporary Ippolitos serve as powerful testaments to the family's enduring qualities: intellect, creativity, resilience, and a drive for excellence.

Consider, for example, the luminous career of **Angelica Ippolito**, born in 1944 in the culturally rich city of Naples, Italy. With her innate charm, captivating stage presence, and profound talent, Angelica captivated and enchanted Italian audiences with her luminous performances across both stage and screen.

From her early roles in gripping dramas to her later comedic turns, her nuanced portrayals brought characters to life with authenticity and warmth. Through her distinctive voice and expressive performances, she skillfully kept alive the deeply emotional and often humorous tradition of Neapolitan storytelling for a modern age, connecting contemporary audiences to a rich cultural heritage. Similarly, **Ciro Ippolito**, born in 1947, also hailing from Naples, carved out a significant career behind the camera. As a versatile director, writer, and producer, Ciro expanded the family's legacy into the dynamic realm of Italian cinema, bridging traditional narrative forms with innovative cinematic techniques. His works, spanning various genres, often explored themes of family, identity, and social commentary, reflecting the depth and complexity inherent in Italian culture, and showcasing the family's artistic inclinations.

Across the vast expanse of the Atlantic, in the vibrant football (soccer) fields of Argentina, young **Dalila Ippolito**, born in 2002, stands as a powerful reminder that a name, imbued with history and pride, can gracefully cross oceans and bridge generations, yet remain an indelible badge of honor. Each time she confidently steps onto the meticulously manicured pitch, whether representing her local club team with fierce determination or proudly donning the national team's jersey, she carries within her veins the very same resilience, passion, and competitive spirit that her ancestors once carried across the challenging waters of the Atlantic. Her burgeoning career symbolizes the global reach of the Ippolito name and its continued impact in diverse fields.

Beyond the captivating worlds of arts and competitive sports, the Ippolito family name continues to flourish brilliantly in the esteemed halls of learning, the rigorous corridors of scientific innovation, and the strategic realms of business and public service. **Dennis Ippolito**, a highly respected American political scientist, has dedicated his career to guiding countless students through the intricate complexities of governance, public policy, and civic life. His scholarly contributions and mentorship have shaped generations of informed citizens and future leaders, embodying the family's commitment to knowledge and public good. **Ian Ippolito**, an American entrepreneur and tech innovator, embodies the family's flair for venturing into new frontiers. With a keen understanding of emerging technologies and market trends, he has successfully built and scaled influential digital platforms that connect people across the globe, showcasing the modern Ippolito drive for ingenuity and connectivity. And in the cutting-edge of profound philosophical circles, **Dr. Joseph A. Ippolito** stands as a testament to the family's intellectual curiosity. His pioneering philosophical work explores the fascinating intersections of electronic imaging, artificial intelligence, and the deep,

often mysterious realms of quantum physics and computing—these pursuits are modern echoes of the family's historic curiosity, intellectual rigor, and unwavering courage in pushing the boundaries of knowledge.

Though each of these stories differs significantly in their chosen paths, their passionate pursuits, and their specific contributions, together they powerfully reaffirm a timeless truth known intrinsically by every Ippolito who came before them: that the truest nobility is not merely measured in ancient titles or inherited wealth, but in the enduring quality of one's deeds, the depth of one's knowledge, the impact of one's innovations, and, most profoundly, in the lasting love, legacy, and positive influence one leaves behind for future generations. The Ippolito name today is a vibrant mosaic of these diverse triumphs, each story adding another brilliant piece to its illustrious history.

"Non si invecchia mai imparando."
— Italian proverb
(One never grows old while learning.)

Tracing Your Branch — *A Practical Guide*

Every family story, however grand or humble, becomes infinitely more meaningful and personally resonant when you can trace precisely where your own life fits within its sprawling, intricate branches. For those who proudly carry the Ippolito name today,

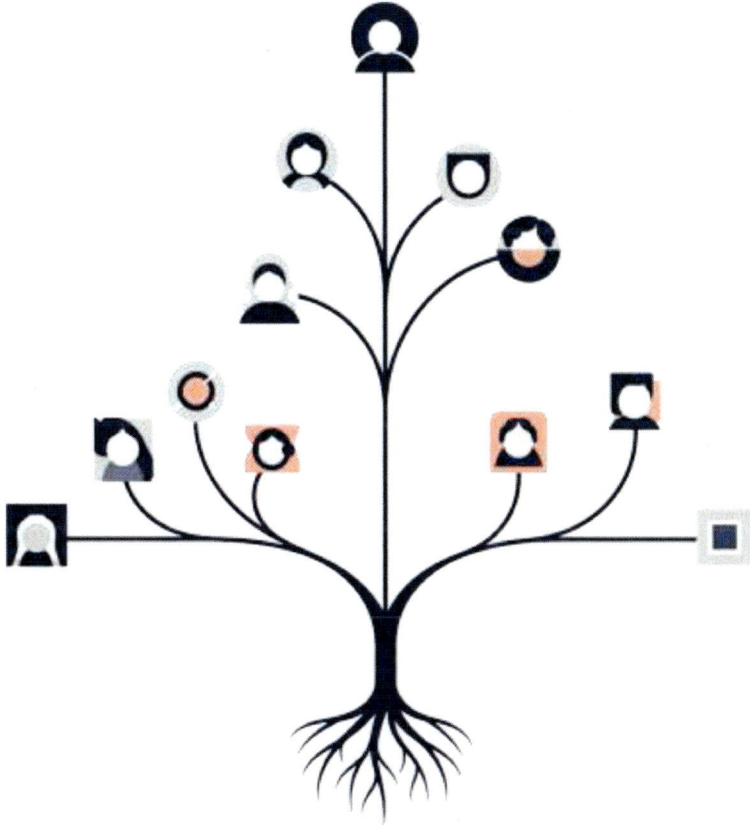

embarking on the journey of researching your lineage is akin to walking an ancient, hallowed footpath, worn smooth by the passage of countless ancestors. It is a deeply personal pilgrimage, a path leading unerringly back through time to the sunlit squares of southern Italy, the cool, quiet stone churches of Sicily, and the timeworn, often dusty archives hidden behind the unassuming doors of charming, historic villages. This journey is not just about names and dates; it is about connecting with the very essence of who you are.

Where, then, does one begin this fascinating quest? The most potent starting point is often the simplest: conversations. Sit patiently and respectfully beside the oldest voices in your family—your beloved parents, cherished grandparents, revered uncles, and dear aunts. These elders are living repositories of invaluable oral history, their memories a precious gift. Ask them not only about names and dates, but also about the towns they remember, the quaint nicknames they heard whispered at the dinner table, the black-and-white photos tucked away in old cedar chests, and the stories behind forgotten traditions. Every anecdote, no matter how seemingly small or insignificant, is a vital thread you can follow back through the labyrinth of time, often unlocking unexpected connections. Document everything: record their voices, write down their stories, and scan those old photographs.

Next, bravely open the metaphorical, and sometimes literal, doors of Italy's ancient parish churches. For centuries, long before the establishment of modern civil registration, it was the local priest who meticulously and faithfully inked each baptism, marriage, and burial into massive, bound registers. These invaluable records, often beautifully handwritten, are still kept safe today in the sacristies and diocesan archives of churches from the bustling metropolis of Naples to the serene, historic streets of Palermo. Many of these ancient books have been painstakingly digitized by genealogical organizations, making them accessible online, or their contents can be formally requested through diocesan archives with the right permissions. Sometimes, a single, elusive record—a mother's maiden name, a specific grandfather's exact village of birth, or a witness's signature—can miraculously unlock generations of forgotten connections, revealing an entire branch of your family tree previously unknown.

Beyond ecclesiastical records, civil archives also hold untold treasures for the persistent researcher. These include formal birth certificates (*atti di nascita*), official marriage acts (*atti di matrimonio*), and precise death records (*atti di morte*), which generally date from the early 1800s onward, when civil registration became mandatory. Modern genealogical websites such as FamilySearch.org (a non-profit, free resource) and Ancestry.com (a subscription-based service) provide millions of indexed Italian records, making it possible to search from the comfort of your home. However, for those with the means and adventurous spirit, visiting local town halls (*comuni*) in Italy may still yield original documents or provide access to local experts who can assist in navigating regional archives. Be prepared for potential language barriers and the charming inefficiencies of Italian bureaucracy, but the reward of holding an original document in your hands is immeasurable.

For the truly adventurous and those facing persistent "brick walls" in their paper trail, a **DNA** test can serve as a powerful modern tool. While not a substitute for traditional genealogical research, DNA testing can reveal hidden branches of your family tree, connect you with distant cousins you never knew existed, and even provide clues about your deep ancestral origins, especially helpful when traditional paper trails fade out or become ambiguous. Finally, and perhaps most profoundly, when your paper trail seems to end, consider making a pilgrimage to your ancestral town. Stand among its ancient stones, walk its narrow, winding streets, and listen to the local dialect carried on the breeze. Visit the church where your ancestors were baptized, the fields they tilled, or the piazza where they gathered. In that moment, you will not only be connecting with history but actively participating in it, knowing that your footsteps complete a powerful, deeply personal circle begun centuries before by those who bore the name Ippolito.

"Chi cerca trova."
— Italian proverb
(Seek, and you shall find.)

Celebrating Our *Living Legacy*

A family name, particularly one as rich and
ancient as Ippolito, survives not merely in brittle
pages of old ledgers or in fading ink on dusty
parchments. Its true vitality, its very essence,
thrives and perpetuates itself in the vibrant
symphony of daily life: in the laughter that drifts
from kitchen windows on a Sunday afternoon, in
the comforting, aromatic scent of simmering
tomato sauce that evokes generations of culinary
tradition, and in the unbroken circle of hands
joined in gratitude at holiday tables. To be an
Ippolito today is not merely to carry an ancient,
honorable name; it is to actively tend a sacred
flame—a living legacy that has burned brightly
through the trials of myth and martyrdom, the
triumphs of nobility, the hardships of migration,
and the enduring human virtues of hope and
resilience.

In an age defined by shrinking distances and remarkable technological advancements that effortlessly connect families across vast continents, perhaps there has never been a more opportune or crucial moment to gather our stories, share our cherished recipes, and consciously pass on the blessings and wisdom whispered by our grandparents. Consider planning a grand family reunion: a joyful weekend where distant cousins, perhaps meeting for the first time, trade worn old photographs for warm new hugs, where the youngest generation learns to pronounce heartfelt **grazie** (thank you) and **per favore** (please) in their ancestral tongue, and where every dish laid out on the expansive table tells a timeless tale older than any one of us. These gatherings are not just social events; they are profound acts of cultural preservation and familial affirmation, weaving new threads into the collective tapestry.

Fill your table with the authentic, beloved foods your ancestors cherished—rustic, comforting pasta dishes fragrant with sun-ripened eggplant and fresh basil; golden, crisp fried rice balls (*arancini*) filled with savory ragù or melted cheese, steaming invitingly from within; and golden loaves of homemade bread, lovingly torn by hand and dipped into fragrant, olive oil pressed from olives grown under the very same southern sun your forebears knew so well. These meals are not just nourishment; they are edible history, a sensory link to the past. Teach each other the traditional songs that echo with the joys and sorrows of generations, the heartfelt toasts that celebrate life and kinship, and the profound prayers that have outlived empires, binding us to a spiritual heritage that transcends time. Share the family anecdotes, the triumphs, the humorous mishaps, and the quiet lessons learned.

As you gather, in these moments of shared joy and connection, remember this profound truth: the Ippolito legacy is not a static relic to be tucked away in an archive or admired from a distance. It is a dynamic, living force that actively manifests in your daily choices, in your acts of kindness and compassion, and in your unwavering resilience when life inevitably grows stormy. It is tangibly present in the comforting stories you tell your children at bedtime, in the quiet, swelling pride you feel when you see your cherished surname on a diploma, a sports jersey, or a letter from a distant relative. It is the wisdom passed down, the values upheld, and the connections forged.

Hold it close, this precious legacy. Pass it on, not just through words, but through lived example. Know that in doing so, you become not merely an heir to a magnificent history, but its vibrant, living, and faithful guardian, ensuring that the Ippolito flame continues to burn brightly for countless generations to come.

"La famiglia è tutto."

(Family is everything.)

📃 Closing *Note*

In these pages, we have embarked on a remarkable journey, tracing the lineage of the Ippolito surname from the hallowed marble temples of ancient *Greece*, where the myth of **Hippolytos** first stirred, to the venerable stone churches of Sicily, where the name found its devout Christian roots. We have traversed bustling piazzas in historic *Naples*, witnessing the daily life of our ancestors, and followed their courageous paths across vast oceans to the vibrant, bustling streets of burgeoning cities like *New York* and the fertile, expansive *Pampas of Buenos Aires*. Along this incredible odyssey, we have encountered a diverse cast of characters: revered *saints*, distinguished *nobles*, hardworking *farmers*, *resilient immigrants*, and innovative *modern trailblazers*—all irrevocably bound by the singular, enduring, and proud name: **Ippolito**.

May this book transcend the mere definition of a keepsake, becoming something far more profound. May it serve as a living guide, a vibrant connection across time—a tangible way to remember the sacrifices and triumphs of those who came before us, to teach the rich narratives and values to future generations, and to collectively celebrate the deep roots and rich heritage from which we all spring. And may every new branch that unfurls from this magnificent family tree flourish with strength and truth, continually nourished by the deep, sustaining roots we honor together, ensuring the Ippolito legacy continues its remarkable journey through time.

Distribution of Ippolitos *Worldwide*

Place	Incidence	Place	Incidence
Italy	12,507	United States	6,115
Argentina	917	France	550
Canada	431	Belgium	285
Brazil	260	Germany	123
Venezuela	116	Australia	106
England	87	Switzerland	86
Dominican Republic	69	Spain	57
Portugal	28	Sweden	14
Colombia	8	Scotland	8
Czechia	7	Denmark	7
Thailand	7	Panama	7
Norway	5	Ireland	4
Romania	4	Ecuador	3
New Zealand	2	Netherlands	2

El Salvador	2	Chile	2
Bolivia	2	Saint Lucia	1
Costa Rica	2	Uruguay	1
Cuba	1	United Arab Emirates	1
Ukraine	1	Cameroon	1
Greece	1	Senegal	1
Hong Kong	1	Saudi Arabia	1
Mexico	1	Russia	1
Israel	1	Puerto Rico	1
Philippines	1	Peru	1
Japan	1	Kazakhstan	1
Nicaragua	1	Luxembourg	1
Malaysia	1	Nepal	1

These are approximate values, and populations change regularly. However, this will give you a pretty good idea of the diaspora of Ippolito *families* in the world. Data gathered by surname.

📄 NOTES on *MY* **Ippolito** *FAMILY*

Thank you so much for joining me on this journey, this exploration of the history of our grand worldwide Italian Ippolito family. I tried to explore the many facets of that which has made Ippolito a special name, one that inspires pride. Whether it is one's given name or their surname, our roots run deep. Now, allow me to proudly share a little bit about my particular branch of the Ippolitos.

My family hales from two different areas in southern Italy: *Torella dei Lombardi* (about 40 kilometers east of Naples) and *Sicily*. It was after World War II that the family migrated to both the United Staes—our branch—as well as to Argentina. In Argentina the family settled in Buenos Aires, and in the United States in the north eastern states of Connecticut, New York and Pennsylvania. There they found work in the steel mills and coal mines of Pennsylvania and the factories of Connecticut, and later New York.

Over the years the diaspora has continued to grow in my branch of the family. Parts of the family relocated in New York from Connecticut. Later they would move on to Florida, and North Carolina. I'm the family's black sheep. I am a true immigrant, I moved on to Costa Rica, Central America, where I currently live.

So, as I researched this book, and spoke with my parents–91 and almost 89 years old–to be clear on our own history, I found out something truly amazing. Where I relocated in Costa Rica is a small *Italo-Costaricano* town in the southern part of the country name **San Vito**. While I was looking into all of the locations of the Ippolitos in Italy, I discovered my family is from *Torella dei Lombardi*, as I mentioned, which is less than 2 kilometers from another small town in Italy named **San Vito**! These are those coincidences in life that one couldn't invent from pure imagination.

Let me share a little bit about our Italian community, San Vito, here in Costa Rica. After the profound upheaval of World War II, Italy found itself grappling with the deep scars of conflict and devastating economic hardship, a land yearning for renewal. In response to the situation, in 1951, the Italian Society for Agricultural Colonization (SICA) was established in Rome, imbuing it with a singular, pioneering mission—to cultivate a verdant agricultural colony upon ten thousand hectares of promising Costa Rican earth. The following year, 1952, saw **Vito Sansonetti** with approximately 150 Italian families, numbering some 500 souls, embark upon a momentous transatlantic voyage, their hearts laden with the longing for a new dawn. Their courageous arrival in Costa Rica heralded the genesis of a community, its very essence forged in resilience and an unyielding spirit of innovation, as these migrants set out to harness the abundant promise of fertile soil and fresh prospects. Upon touching Costa Rican soil, they began to meticulously lay the bedrock for what would burgeon into the thriving settlement of *San Vito*. This indomitable will and concerted effort transmuted a remote, untamed expanse into a vibrant, self-sustaining community.

Through the crucible of time, San Vito blossomed into a profound cultural nucleus, a place where the cherished traditions of Italy gracefully blended with the vibrant hues of local customs, leaving an indelible legacy that profoundly enriches Costa Rica's social and agricultural landscape even to this very day.

As for the rest of our family's diaspora, as far as I have been able to ascertain, beyond Italy, the United States and Argentina, I understand that our branch of the family also extends to France and Switzerland.

In a final tribute to my parents and grandparents, I am proud to include the following photographs.

My Grandparents

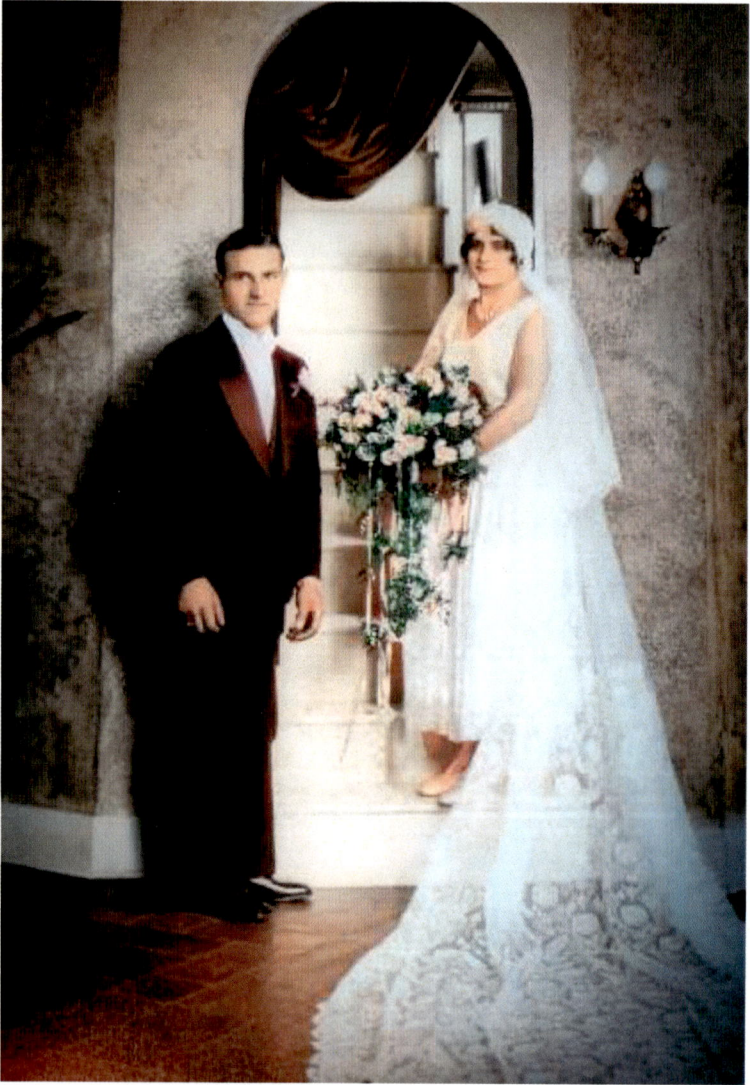

Giuseppe (Joseph) Ippolito & Elvira (Pisano) Ippolito

My Parents

Vincent Ippolito & Helen (Maccalous) Ippolito

Grandparents & Parents

From left to right:

(Domenico Giuseppe) Michael Joseph Maccalous
(Macaluso) *Grandfather*

(Rosaria) Rose Isabel (Di Martino) Maccalous
Grandmother

Helen Esther (Maccalous) Ippolito
Mother

Vincent Joseph Ippolito
Father

Elvira Pasqualina (Pisano) Ippolito
Grandmother

(Giuseppe) Joseph Anthony Ippolito
Grandfather

As frequently occurs, many names and surnames were
anglicized in America.

Acknowledgments

To the countless Ippolitos, both past and present, whose quiet courage, unwavering determination, and profound love built this extraordinary legacy—your silent contributions resonate deeply through these pages. And to those yet unborn, who will carry this torch forward with fresh dreams, new achievements, and renewed spirit—may you find inspiration in these stories. To Vincent and Helen Ippolito, my beloved parents, and the primary guardians of our family's vibrant memory; and to all our grandparents, great-grandparents, and every individual who, through their lives and their stories, contributed to the preservation of our collective memory—your dedication and love are the bedrock of this book. Thank you, from the deepest part of my heart, for making this narrative possible.

Traditional *Recipes*

Here are a few beloved recipes, simple yet profoundly timeless, that might have graced an Ippolito table in the sun-drenched kitchens of Sicily or the rustic homes of Torella dei Lombardi or Calabria generations ago. These dishes are more than food; they are a taste of heritage, a culinary connection to our ancestors.

Basic Southern Italian Pasta Dough

(Semola & Water)

This is a versatile dough, often found in regions like Puglia, Basilicata, Calabria, and even Campania (Naples), where a harder, chewier texture is preferred, and eggs were traditionally saved for richer dishes. While true commercial "spaghetti" is extruded, many southern Italian *nonnas* create similar long, thin pasta by hand-rolling and cutting, or by shaping processes that produce a rustic, irregular strand.

Yields: 4 servings (approx. 250-300g pasta)
Prep time: 30 minutes dough making + 30 minutes rest + shaping time
Cook time: 5-8 minutes for fresh pasta

Ingredients:

- 200g (approx. 1 ½ cups) **Durum Wheat Semolina Flour** (*semola rimacinata di grano duro* - this is finely milled durum wheat, essential for texture)
- 100ml (approx. ½ cup) **Warm Water** (plus a little extra, as needed)
- A pinch of **Fine Sea Salt** (optional, many traditionalists omit it for pasta dough as the cooking water is salted)

Equipment:

- Large clean work surface (wooden board is traditional and best)
- Dough scraper (optional, but very helpful for cleaning and mixing)

- Bench knife or sharp knife (for cutting dough)
- Rolling pin (optional, if you want to roll out sheets for cutting)

Instructions:

1. **Form the Well (La Fontana):** On your clean work surface, pour the semolina into a neat mound. Create a deep well in the center of the mound, like a volcano crater, with high walls.
2. **Combine Wet and Dry:** Pour the warm water (and salt, if using) into the center of the well.
3. **Mix Gradually:** Using your fingers or a fork, slowly incorporate the flour from the inner walls of the well into the water. Continue to mix until a shaggy, wet dough begins to form.
4. **Knead:** As the dough comes together, start kneading with your hands. Gather all the flour into the mass. Knead firmly and energetically for at least 10-15 minutes.
   - **Hydration Check:** The dough should feel firm but pliable, smooth, and elastic. It should not be sticky. If it feels too dry and crumbly, add water a teaspoon at a time. If too sticky, add a tiny sprinkle of

semolina. The final dough should be quite firm.

- o *Granny Wisdom:* "The dough will tell you what it needs." Pay attention to its texture. The extensive kneading develops the gluten in the durum wheat, which gives the pasta its characteristic chew.

5. **Rest the Dough:** Form the dough into a ball, cover it tightly with an overturned bowl or plastic wrap, and let it rest at room temperature for a minimum of 30 minutes (longer is fine, up to an hour or two). This resting period allows the gluten to relax, making the dough much easier to roll and shape.

To Shape "Spaghetti-like" Strands (Hand-Rolled/Cut):

- **Roll into Ropes:** Take a portion of the rested dough (keep the rest covered). On a lightly floured surface (use semolina), roll the dough into a very long, thin rope, aiming for the desired thickness of spaghetti. You can do this by hand, or by rolling out a thin sheet and then cutting it.
- **Cut into Strands:**
  - o **Method 1 (Rustic Hand-Cut):** If you've made a rope, you can carefully cut thin strands from it

with a sharp knife, or even try the "dragging" technique used for Pici or some other hand-rolled pastas where you roll a piece of dough directly into a strand.

- o **Method 2 (Sheet and Cut):** Roll the dough into a thin sheet (about 1-2mm thickness, similar to a lasagna sheet). Lightly dust with semolina, then fold the sheet over several times or roll it loosely into a log. Using a sharp knife, cut thin strips (around 2mm wide) from the folded sheet or log. Unfurl the strands gently.
- **Dry Slightly:** Lay the freshly cut pasta strands on a lightly floured surface (again, semolina is best) or a clean tea towel. Let

them dry for 15-30 minutes before cooking. This helps them hold their shape and prevents sticking.

Cooking:

1. Bring a large pot of generously salted water to a rolling boil.
2. Add the fresh pasta and cook for 5-8 minutes, or until *al dente* (firm to the bite). Fresh pasta cooks *very quickly*, so keep an eye on it.
3. Drain, reserving some pasta water, and toss immediately with your favorite sauce. For a Southern Italian touch, a simple tomato sauce, a garlic and oil (aglio e olio) sauce, or a light seafood sauce would be perfect.

This basic dough is the foundation for countless Southern Italian pasta shapes and provides a truly authentic homemade pasta experience.

Eggplant Parmesan
(or *Parmigiana di Melanzane*)

Eggplant Parmigiana is a beloved staple of Southern Italian cuisine, with roots primarily in Campania and Sicily. While there are many family variations, the core elements remain consistent for a truly traditional taste.

Here's a general guide to a classic Southern Italian Eggplant Parmigiana:

Key Characteristics of a *Traditional Southern Italian Version*:

- **Fried Eggplant:** The eggplant slices are almost always fried, not baked or grilled, which gives the dish its rich, unctuous texture. Many traditional recipes advise salting the eggplant slices first to draw out bitterness and excess moisture, then rinsing and patting them dry before frying. Some even suggest lightly dusting them in flour, or flour and egg, before frying.

- **Simple Tomato Sauce:** The sauce is typically a straightforward tomato sauce (*sugo (ragù) al pomodoro*), often made with good quality canned whole tomatoes (like San Marzano), garlic, and fresh basil. It's usually cooked until it's not too watery.

- **Cheese:** Mozzarella (often fresh, but sometimes low-moisture shredded or even provolone/caciocavallo in certain regional variations) and grated Parmigiano-Reggiano (or sometimes Pecorino Romano for a sharper flavor) are the cheeses of choice.

- **No Breading (usually):** Unlike many American versions, *traditional Italian* Eggplant Parmigiana *rarely uses breadcrumbs* as a coating for the eggplant or layered within the dish.
- **Optional Additions:** Some regional variations, particularly in parts of Campania or Puglia, might include a thin layer of cooked ham or mortadella between the layers.

Simplified Steps for a Traditional Approach:

1. Prepare the Eggplant:
   - Slice medium eggplants (often the long, purple variety) into about 1/4 to 1/2-inch thick slices.
   - Generously salt both sides of the slices and lay them in a colander. Place a plate and a weight on top to press out excess water and bitterness. Let them drain for at least an hour, or even overnight in the fridge.
   - Rinse the salted eggplant slices thoroughly under cold water to remove excess salt, then pat them completely dry with kitchen towels.
   - Fry the eggplant slices in batches in hot vegetable oil (like peanut or sunflower oil) until golden brown

and tender. Drain them on paper towels to remove excess oil.

2. **Make a *Simple Tomato Sauce*:**
   - Sauté a little garlic (and sometimes finely diced onion or carrot) in olive oil.
   - Add good quality crushed or pureed canned tomatoes (San Marzano are highly recommended).
   - Season with salt, pepper, and fresh basil leaves. Simmer for at least 30-60 minutes until it thickens slightly.

3. **Assemble the Parmigiana:**
   - Preheat your oven (around 350-375°F / 175-190°C).
   - Lightly spread a ladleful of tomato sauce on the bottom of a baking dish.
   - Arrange a single layer of fried eggplant slices over the sauce.
   - Top the eggplant with another thin layer of tomato sauce, fresh basil leaves (torn), slices or cubes of mozzarella, and a generous sprinkle of grated Parmigiano-Reggiano.
   - Repeat the layers until all ingredients are used, ending with a layer of sauce and a generous dusting of Parmigiano-Reggiano on top.

4. Bake:

- Bake uncovered for 30-40 minutes, or until the sauce is bubbling, and the cheese is melted and golden brown on top.
- Let it rest for at least 10-15 minutes before serving to allow the layers to set and the flavors to meld. This dish is often even better served warm or at room temperature.

Sicilian Cannoli

These iconic Sicilian pastries, with their crisp, fried shells and creamy, sweet ricotta filling, are a testament to the island's vibrant dessert tradition.

Ingredients:

- For the Shells
  (or use good quality store-bought):

- 2 cups all-purpose flour
- 2 tablespoons granulated sugar
- 1/2 teaspoon unsweetened cocoa powder (for color and subtle flavor)
- 1/2 teaspoon ground cinnamon (optional)
- Pinch of salt
- 2 tablespoons cold unsalted butter, cut into small pieces
- 1 large egg yolk
- 1/2 cup dry Marsala wine (or white wine/grape juice for non-alcoholic version)
- Vegetable oil or shortening for deep frying (about 4-6 cups)

For the Filling:

- 2 lbs fresh ricotta cheese (full-fat, preferably sheep's milk ricotta), well-drained for at least 4-6 hours, or overnight, in a sieve lined with cheesecloth in the refrigerator. This is critical for thick, non-soggy filling.
- 1 1/2 cups powdered sugar (confectioners' sugar), or to taste
- 1 teaspoon vanilla extract
- 1/2 cup mini chocolate chips, finely chopped dark chocolate, or finely diced candied fruit (e.g., orange peel, citron, cherries) – traditional additions
- Optional: 1/4 cup chopped pistachios for decorating ends

Instructions:

1. **Prepare the Shells (if homemade):** In a large bowl, whisk together the flour, sugar, cocoa powder, cinnamon (if using), and salt. Cut in the cold butter using your fingertips or a pastry blender until the mixture resembles coarse crumbs. Add the egg yolk and Marsala wine. Mix until a shaggy dough forms, then turn it out onto a lightly floured surface. Knead for about 5-7 minutes until the dough is smooth and elastic. Wrap in plastic wrap and refrigerate for at least 30 minutes, or up to 2 hours.

2. **Roll and Cut Dough:** On a lightly floured surface, roll the chilled dough very thinly (about 1/16-inch thick). You can use a pasta machine for best results, rolling it progressively thinner. Using a 3-4 inch round cookie cutter, cut out circles. Reshape dough scraps gently and re-roll.

3. **Form and Fry Shells:** Heat vegetable oil in a deep, heavy-bottomed pot or Dutch oven to 350° F / 175 °. Lightly grease cannoli forms (metal tubes). Wrap each dough circle around a cannoli form, overlapping the ends slightly and sealing with a dab of egg white or water. Fry 2-3 shells at a time, turning occasionally, until golden brown and crisp, about 1-2

minutes. Using tongs, carefully remove the hot shells and place them on paper towels to drain. Once cool enough to handle, gently slide the forms out of the shells. Let shells cool completely before filling.

4. **Prepare the Filling:** In a large bowl, combine the well-drained ricotta cheese, powdered sugar, and vanilla extract. Beat with an electric mixer on medium speed (or by hand with a whisk) until the mixture is completely smooth, creamy, and light. If desired, gently fold in the mini chocolate chips, chopped chocolate, or candied fruit. Do not overmix once the additions are in.

5. **Fill the Cannoli:** *This is important*: **Fill the cannoli shells just before serving.** If filled too early, the shells will absorb moisture from the ricotta and become soggy. Using a pastry bag fitted with a large round tip (or a spoon), pipe or spoon the ricotta filling into each end of the cooled cannoli shells until they are completely filled.

6. **Garnish and Serve:** Dust the filled cannoli with extra powdered sugar. For traditional presentation, you can dip the ends in chopped pistachios or additional mini chocolate chips. Enjoy immediately with a strong espresso or a glass of sweet Marsala wine.

Zeppole di San Giuseppe

Zeppole are delightful Italian pastries, especially popular in Southern Italy, particularly Campania, and traditionally enjoyed on St. Joseph's Day (March 19th). They are essentially a fried (or sometimes baked) choux pastry, often filled with a luscious pastry cream (*crema pasticcera*) and garnished with a candied cherry and a dusting of powdered sugar.

Zeppole di San Giuseppe (Fried with Pastry Cream)

This recipe makes about 10-12 medium-sized zeppole.

Crema Pasticcera (Pastry Cream)

Ingredients:

- 2 cups (480ml) whole milk
- 1/2 vanilla bean, split lengthwise, or 1 tsp vanilla extract
- 4 large egg yolks
- 1/2 cup (100g) granulated sugar
- 1/4 cup (30g) all-purpose flour or 2 tablespoons cornstarch (cornstarch makes a slightly lighter cream)
- 2 tablespoons (28g) unsalted butter, cut into small pieces

Instructions:

1. **Infuse Milk:** In a medium saucepan, combine the milk and the split vanilla bean (if using vanilla extract, add it later). Heat over medium-low heat until it just begins to simmer, but do not boil. Remove from heat and let steep for 5-10 minutes to infuse the vanilla flavor. Remove the vanilla bean pod.

2. **Whisk Yolks and Sugar:** In a medium bowl, whisk together the egg yolks and sugar until pale yellow and slightly fluffy.

3. **Add Flour/Cornstarch:** Whisk in the flour or cornstarch until well combined and no lumps remain.

4. **Temper Egg Mixture:** Gradually and slowly pour about 1/2 cup of the hot milk into the egg yolk mixture while whisking constantly. This "tempers" the eggs, preventing them from scrambling.

5. **Combine and Cook:** Pour the tempered egg mixture back into the saucepan with the remaining hot milk. Return the saucepan to medium-low heat and cook, whisking constantly, until the mixture thickens significantly and a few bubbles pop on the surface. This will take about 3-5 minutes. The cream should be thick enough to coat the back of a spoon.

6. **Add Butter and Strain:** Remove from heat and whisk in the butter until it's completely melted and incorporated, making the cream smooth and glossy. For an even smoother cream, you can press it through a fine-mesh sieve into a clean bowl.

7. **Cool:** Cover the surface of the pastry cream directly with plastic wrap (to prevent a skin from forming) and refrigerate until completely chilled, at least 4 hours, or preferably overnight. The cream needs to be cold and firm for piping.

Choux Pastry (Pâte à Choux) for Zeppole

Ingredients:

- 1 cup (240ml) water

- 1/2 cup (113g) unsalted butter, cut into pieces

- 1 tablespoon (15g) granulated sugar (optional, for golden color)

- 1/2 teaspoon fine sea salt

- 1 cup (120g) all-purpose flour, sifted

- 4 large eggs, at room temperature

Instructions:

1. **Prepare Base:** In a large saucepan, combine the water, butter, sugar (if using), and salt. Bring the mixture to a rolling boil over medium-high heat, stirring until the butter is completely melted.

2. **Add Flour:** Once boiling, remove the pan from the heat and immediately add all the sifted flour at once. Stir vigorously with a wooden spoon until the mixture comes together and forms a smooth ball of dough that pulls away from the sides of the pan.

3. **Cook Dough:** Return the pan to medium heat and continue stirring for 1-2 minutes to dry out the dough slightly. This step is crucial for light and airy zeppole. A thin film will form on the bottom of the pan.

4. **Cool Slightly:** Transfer the dough to a large mixing bowl (or the bowl of a stand mixer fitted with a paddle attachment). Spread it out a bit to help it cool for about 5 minutes.

5. **Incorporate Eggs:** Add the eggs one at a time, beating well after each addition until fully incorporated before adding the next egg. The dough will look separated and lumpy at first, but keep mixing, and it will come together into a smooth, shiny, and thick paste. The final dough should be a "V" shape when lifted with a spoon.

6. **Prepare for Frying:** Transfer the choux pastry to a large piping bag fitted with a large open star tip (such as an Ateco 826 or 1M).

Frying and Assembly

Ingredients:

- Vegetable oil or peanut oil, for deep frying

- Powdered sugar, for dusting

- Amarena cherries in syrup, for garnish (or maraschino cherries)

Instructions:

1. **Heat Oil:** Pour about 2-3 inches of vegetable oil into a deep, heavy-bottomed pot or Dutch oven. Heat the oil to 350°F (175°C). Use a candy thermometer to monitor the temperature.

2. **Pipe Zeppole:** You can either pipe the zeppole directly into the hot oil or pipe them onto small squares of parchment paper first, then carefully drop the parchment paper with the dough into the oil (the parchment will peel away easily in the hot oil).

   o To pipe directly: Hold the piping bag about 1 inch above the oil and pipe rings or spirals, about 2.5-3 inches in diameter. You can also pipe small mounds if you prefer a puff shape.

- Work in batches, being careful not to overcrowd the pot, as this will lower the oil temperature.

3. **Fry Zeppole:** Fry the zeppole for about 4-6 minutes per side, or until they are deeply golden brown and puffed up. Flip them gently with tongs or a slotted spoon to ensure even cooking.

4. **Drain:** Once golden, remove the zeppole from the oil and place them on a wire rack lined with paper towels to drain excess oil. Let them cool completely.

5. **Fill Zeppole:** Once the zeppole are cool, retrieve your chilled pastry cream. If it's too firm, whisk it briefly to loosen it slightly. Transfer the pastry cream to a piping bag fitted with a star tip (or a plain round tip).

   - **Method 1 (Cutting):** Carefully cut each zeppola in half horizontally using a serrated knife. Pipe a generous amount of pastry cream onto the bottom half, then place the top half back on.

   - **Method 2 (Piping through)** *recommended*: For a cleaner look, you can sometimes gently poke a hole in the bottom or side of the zeppola with a small knife or the piping tip, then pipe the cream directly into the center until it feels full.

6. **Garnish and Serve:** Dust the assembled zeppole generously with powdered sugar. Place an Amarena cherry (or a few small pieces) on top of each zeppola. Serve immediately for the best texture and flavor.

Enjoy these classic Southern Italian treats!

Author's note:

We made Zeppole differently, much more *rustically*. In our home, we simple took any leftover pizza or bread dough, and tore it into pieces to be fried as dessert. This was topped with powdered sugar, for appearance as well as a touch of sweetness. *Presto-presto!*

Other Suggested *Recipes to Explore*

Arancini di Riso (Sicilian Rice Balls):

Golden, crispy fried rice balls, typically stuffed with ragù (meat sauce), mozzarella, and peas, then deep-fried to perfection. A popular street food and appetizer.

Pasta alla Norma (Pasta with Tomato, Eggplant, and Ricotta Salata):

A truly iconic Sicilian pasta dish from Catania. It features short pasta (like rigatoni or macaroni) tossed in a rich tomato sauce, served with fried eggplant cubes, and generously topped with grated *ricotta salata* (salted, aged ricotta cheese). Simple, yet incredibly flavorful.

Limoncello (Homemade Lemon Liqueur — *optional family treat*):

While not a 'food', this vibrant, sweet, and tangy lemon liqueur is a quintessential Italian *digestivo*, particularly popular in Southern Italy. Made from lemon zest, sugar, and alcohol, it's often made at home and shared after meals, embodying the spirit of Italian hospitality.

These cherished recipes, passed down through the whispers of generations, are more than mere instructions; they are a direct line to our heritage. For an Ippolito, keeping our vibrant culture alive isn't just important; **it is regarded as a sacred duty**, and as we all know, there's no better sacrament than a truly magnificent meal! To us Italians, food is far more than just eating or nourishment. It's the very glue of our existence, binding families, forging friendships, and cementing the bonds of neighborhood with every shared bite. The delightful recipes I've had the pleasure of sharing here aren't strictly from one family's secret vault, but rather a joyful symphony of Southern Italian variations, harmonized from countless kitchens. And let's be honest, whatever your personal 'Nonna's secret' twist may be, you *know* deep down it's unequivocally the best version, superior to all others... *right?* If you just nodded vigorously, perhaps even with a dramatic flourish of the hand, then congratulations, you are undeniably, wonderfully, an **Ippolito** through and through!

References & Further Reading

- Dictionary of American Family Names, Oxford University Press
- Archives of Mantua, Pistoia, Naples, and Palermo (historical documents, civic records, and ecclesiastical registers)
- Forebears.io surname database (for global surname distribution and historical data)
- Heraldry Institute of Rome reports (for insights into Italian coats of arms and noble lineages)
- FamilySearch.org and Ancestry.com Italian record collections (online genealogical databases for civil and parish records)
- Personal oral histories and family records (interviews with family members, private documents, letters, and photographs)
- *The Italian Americans: A History* by Jerre Mangione and Ben Morreale
- Blood of My Blood: The Dilemma of the Italian-Americans by Richard Gambino
- *A History of Sicily* by Denis Mack Smith

If you liked this book, and *you can read Italian*, you may like my other books:

L'Arte della Parola:

Prosa descrittiva che mette in mostra la bellezza e la potenza della lingua italiana stessa, il suo ritmo e la sua capacità di catturare l'essenza della vita. (2024)

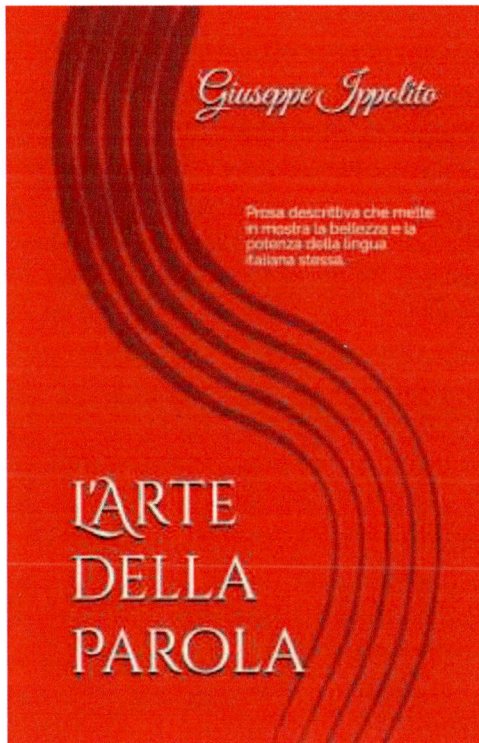

Viaggio alla scoperta della bellezza della lingua italiana. Se ami l'Italia e sei affascinato dalla musicalità e dalle sfumature infinite della sua lingua, questo libro farà al caso tuo. Attraverso pagine ricche di descrizioni suggestive e vivaci analisi linguistiche, l'autore ti accompagnerà in un viaggio emozionante lungo lo Stivale, alla scoperta dei tanti aspetti che rendono l'italiano unico. Dai sapori intensi della cucina regionale alle leggende sussurrate in dialetto, dai proverbi che racchiudono saggezza secolare alle feste popolari che colorano le strade con gioia travolgente, ogni capitolo è un'esperienza sensoriale che ti farà immergere nella cultura e nell'anima di questo meraviglioso Paese. Imparerai a "leggere" non solo le parole ma anche i gesti eloquenti e i silenzi densi di significato che caratterizzano la comunicazione italiana. Scoprirai come la lingua catturi l'essenza di ciò che ci circonda, dalla bellezza dei paesaggi ai momenti più preziosi rubati al tempo. Divertendoti con curiosità ed esercizi, perfezionerai il tuo italiano e aumenterai la tua comprensione di usi e costumi. Questo libro è la guida ideale per tutti coloro che vogliono innamorarsi ancora di più dell'Italia e della sua lingua unica. Un viaggio che ti lascerà desideroso di continuare ad esplorare. Cosa aspetti? Immergiti nella magia dell'italiano e preparati a rimanere incantato!

PAGINE AL CHIARO DI LUNA: RACCONTI POETICI SOTTO LA TELA CELESTE

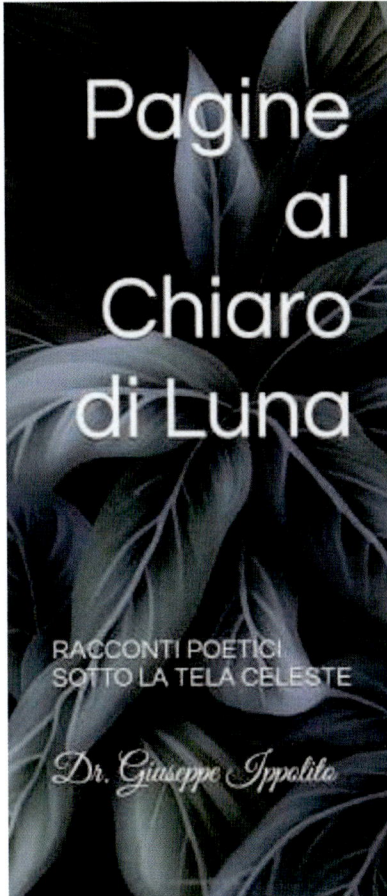

(2023)

Lasciati trasportare dalla poesia di Giuseppe Antonio Ippolito in un viaggio poetico sotto il manto delle stelle. In queste pagine scoprirai città dimenticate prese d'assalto dall'immaginazione, innamorati le cui storie si intrecciano con la luce lunare, e antichi segreti custoditi dalle costellazioni. I versi dell'autore ti condurranno in territori incantati, tra atmosfere suggestive e riflessioni sull'animo umano. Una raccolta ideale per gli amanti della poesia e per chi desidera immergersi nella bellezza e nel mistero delle ore notturne. Un tuffo in un universo poetico che si svela poesia dopo poesia, in cui fantasia e sentimento si fondono sotto il cielo stellato.

About the Author

Dr. (Giuseppe Antonio) Joseph Anthony Ippolito defies easy categorization. A researcher, author, and academic, his intellectual pursuits span both the scientific and artistic realms. His published works demonstrate extraordinary breadth, including books on the philosophy of quantum physics, artificial intelligence and bio-computing, electronic imaging, fiction, philosophical treatises, and numerous volumes of poetry. He writes and publishes in English, Spanish, and Italian.

Beyond the written word, Dr. Ippolito is also an acclaimed visual artist whose work has been exhibited internationally.

His scholarly articles appear in academic journals around the globe.

His poetry in English, Spanish, and Italian complements his cross-cultural literary output.

This remarkable diversity reflects his lifelong commitment to pushing boundaries and exploring the full spectrum of human thought and creativity.

Dr. Ippolito's contributions enrich a wide array of fields. A true Renaissance mind, he uses his multifaceted talents to illuminate the world for readers, viewers, and fellow scholars alike.

Notes About **YOUR** IPPOLITO FAMILY!

Feel free to use the back of this book for keeping the Ippolito legacy alive, through family stories, recipes, or anything you value, being an Ippolito!

_____

_____

_____

_____

_____

_____

_____

IPPOLITO

Ippolito

"Borne from myth, baptized in faith, and tempered by time, The name Ippolito moves like wind through olive trees—whispering of lions, ships, and sacred soil. It does not fade; it roots itself in memory, blossoming anew where hearts remain brave and true."

—Giuseppe Ippolito, 2025

Made in United States
Orlando, FL
19 June 2025